THE MSS

THE MSS

ODYSSEYS

C. C. ANTON

CREATIVE EDUCATION · CREATIVE PAPERBACKS

Published by Creative Education and Creative Paperbacks
P.O. Box 227, Mankato, Minnesota 56002
Creative Education and Creative Paperbacks
are imprints of The Creative Company
www.thecreativecompany.us

Design by Graham Morgan
Art direction by Tom Morgan
Edited by Jill Kalz

Images by Associated Press/Charles Tasnadi, 52; Getty Images,/Kemter, 44, Mirrorpix, 61, TIM SLOAN, 56, Universal History Archive, 20, -/XINHUA/AFP, 34–35; Shutterstock/Atstock Productions, 2, Bartosz Luczak, 26, BeeBright, 48, Fer Gregory, 28, Hung Chung Chih, 12, pixinoo, 8; Unsplash/Aaron Greenwood, 4–5, Gigi, 14, Hanny Naibaho, 39, Jürgen Jester, 24, Matthieu Beaumont, 75, Solen Feyissa, 64; Wikimedia Commons/ Dati Bendo, 70, Department of Defense, 69, public domain, 11, 19, 31, 51, Rinatulino, cover, 6

Library of Congress Cataloging-in-Publication Data
Names: Anton, C. C., author.
Title: The MSS / C. C. Anton.
Description: Mankato, Minnesota : Creative Education and Creative Paperbacks, [2025] | Series: Odysseys in Spycraft | Includes bibliographical references and index. | Audience: Ages 12–15 | Audience: Grades 7–9 | Summary: "Unlock the spy secrets of China's (MSS), from the civilian espionage agency's history of intelligence gathering to training and key missions. Includes a glossary, sidebars, index, and further resources"—Provided by publisher.
Identifiers: LCCN 2024018508 (print) | LCCN 2024018509 (ebook) | ISBN 9798889892953 (library binding) | ISBN 9781682776612 (paperback) | ISBN 9798889894063 (ebook)
Subjects: LCSH: Intelligence service—China—Juvenile literature. | Secret service—China—Juvenile literature.
Classification: LCC JQ1509.5.I6 A58 2025 (print) | LCC JQ1509.5.I6 (ebook) | DDC 327.1251—dc23/eng/20240513
LC record available at https://lccn.loc.gov/2024018508
LC ebook record available at https://lccn.loc.gov/2024018509

Printed in the United States of America

Seal of the Ministry of State Security

CONTENTS

FEMALE
BROWN HAI
AFRICAN
RELAXED
BAG
4876592
N HAIR
ASIAN
SED
ID : 548765942
MALE
GREY HAIR
CAUCASIAN
RELAXED
BAG
TIFICATION : ON - OBJECTS DETECTIO

Introduction

The tale of Chinese **espionage** began thousands of years ago, rooted in ancient methods of spying and secret operations. Throughout the history of the territory known today as China, leaders have used spies to gather **intelligence**. This information, collected about enemy rulers, governments, and their troops, is often used for strategic military, political, and economic reasons.

OPPOSITE: Today's technology allows spies to easily gather information about people and target potential threats.

OPPOSITE Sun Tzu advised people to keep their friends close and their enemies closer.

The famous Chinese military strategist Sun Tzu wrote *The Art of War* around the 5th-century B.C.E., more than 2,500 years ago. The entire final chapter of this classic text covers spying, intelligence gathering, and espionage. Sun Tzu offers suggestions on how to use different kinds of intelligence to gain an upper hand over one's enemies. Sun Tzu advised, "One who knows the enemy and knows himself will not be endangered in a hundred engagements."

The Art of War remains one of the most influential books on military strategy ever written. But it wasn't the only book of its kind. There are six other ancient Chinese military texts. Together, they are known as

中国武警

OPPOSITE No country in the world has a larger army than China.

the Seven Military Classics. They provide a glimpse into some of the earliest intelligence operations and tradecraft ever recorded.

The legacy of ancient Chinese espionage still influences and guides the country's intelligence community today. It laid the groundwork for future intelligence services of China and eventually led to the foundation of the modern-day Ministry of State Security (MSS).

Shadows of the Past

Long ago, before the era of **imperial dynasties** in Chinese history, systems of government in the region varied a lot. The Zhou dynasty (1046 B.C.E.–256 B.C.E.) is considered the second dynasty in the study of traditional Chinese history. During this time, China was ruled by a centralized **monarchy**. The king granted land to people in exchange for their loyalty. It is worth noting that Sun Tzu wrote *The Art of War* during this time.

OPPOSITE: The Forbidden City, a palace complex in Beijing erected during the Ming dynasty, was the center of power in China for more than 500 years.

The Zhou dynasty was short-lived compared with later dynasties, but the king was extremely powerful during this period. However, over time, the power of the central monarchy weakened significantly, leaving the king with less and less power over the people. This led to the eventual collapse of the Zhou dynasty. The period after the dynasty's fall is often referred to as the "Warring States Period" (475 B.C.E.–221 B.C.E.). It was an age characterized by intense warfare and political division throughout all of present-day China. Instead of one central government, there were many smaller groups called states, each with their own leaders and laws, fighting one another for control and power.

During the Warring States Period, rival states frequently employed spies. These spies gathered intelligence on movements of enemy troops, their military strategies, and their future plans. They operated in secrecy and often risked their lives to serve their lords and kingdoms.

One of the warring states, the Qin state, was led by Qin Shi Huang. He was 38 years old when he came into power. He is credited with coining the term "emperor" for himself. That's why he's often referred to as the first emperor of China. Qin Shi Huang ultimately defeated all the other states and successfully unified China under one central government in 221 B.C.E. The move marked the end of the Warring States Period and the beginning of the dynastic period of Chinese history.

Qin Shi Huang frequently relied on spies, espionage, and other intelligence gathering techniques to accomplish his goals. Sometimes, his spies acted as **double agents**, pretending to be loyal to enemy states but secretly working for the Qin dynasty. This allowed the spies to gather valuable intelligence while also deceiving their enemies about the true intentions and capabilities of the Qin forces.

In addition to these offensive tactics, the Qin dynasty relied on the use of **counterespionage** measures to protect its own secrets. These defensive measures also helped prevent enemies from gaining secret access to the Qin dynasty's military. Tactics included screening officials and advisors for loyalty, maintaining **surveillance** on potential threats, and using **encryption** methods to maintain the secrecy of potentially sensitive or damaging communications.

Qin Shi Huang, protected by his traveling entourage

Kang Sheng [*right*] discusses plans with Mao Zedong.

Terror of Kang

Kang Sheng was one of the most powerful figures in the CCP during the Chinese Civil War. He worked closely with Chairman Mao Zedong, the first leader of the PRC from its founding in 1949 until his death in 1976. Kang was a ruthless leader. The fear instilled by his violent, brutal tactics created a culture of obedience and conformity across the nation. People became used to accepting the desires of the state in order to avoid punishment or death. Kang Sheng's "legacy of terror" has had a lasting impact on the Chinese people's willingness to comply with the wishes of the Chinese government.

Intelligence gathering underwent notable changes as China transitioned into modern times. The country's final imperial dynasty, the Qing dynasty, fell in 1912. The resulting establishment of the Republic of China marked the beginning of a new era of intelligence operations. Both of the country's major political forces, the Nationalists and the **Communists**, built advanced spy networks during the Chinese Civil War (1927–49). They used **covert** methods to gain strategic advantages over one another. When the Chinese Communist Party (CCP) finally won the war in 1949, they created the People's Republic of China (PRC).

Lessons learned from the long civil war highlighted the importance of having one primary intelligence agency. So, in 1955, the PRC set up the Ministry of Public Security (MPS) to handle security matters inside the country. It wasn't until 1983 that the Chinese government officially formed the MSS as its primary civilian intelligence agency. The agency was formed by merging the espionage, counterespionage, and security functions of the MPS with the Investigations Department of the CCP Central Committee. Several complex and multi-layered factors led to its development, including the need to consolidate power and stabilize the government, to keep up with advancements in technology, and to focus on gathering secret economic information from other countries.

Led by veteran intelligence officers and highly skilled **agents**, the MSS became the official agency in charge of China's intelligence service. It was responsible for both domestic and foreign intelligence operations. Under Chinese leaders who came after Chairman Mao Zedong, the MSS grew and changed. Today, it is still leading China's efforts to protect national security and achieve the goals of the PRC.

The Chinese approach to intelligence gathering is quite different from the approach that Russia and most Western countries take. The PRC defines intelligence practices in ways that often overlap with the unconventional methods described in ancient military texts such as *The Art of War*. However, it's important to note that

OPPOSITE Public surveillance cameras throughout China constantly record people's movements and activities.

there are major differences between what is outlined in those ancient texts and China's modern-day stance on espionage. While the ancient texts openly discuss such strategies, today's intelligence activities are much more secretive. The Chinese government closely guards its state secrets. Little is known about the MSS compared to, for example, the Committee for State Security (KGB) in Russia, the Central Intelligence Agency (CIA) in the United States, or the Security Service (MI5) in the United Kingdom.

MSS Tactics

There are many details about the MSS that remain shrouded in secrecy—so many that it almost sounds like something out of a Hollywood movie. The location of its headquarters is unknown. The number of employees is classified. The identities of many officials and key personnel are kept hidden. The MSS has no public website and no press office. Its budget is unknown but presumed to have few limitations.

OPPOSITE: Anonymity is one of the MSS's greatest strengths.

Locked Up

It is believed that the MSS operates several jail-like facilities across China. Individuals accused of **dissenting** against the communist government are reportedly subjected to harsh treatment. Tactics include alleged violations of fundamental human rights as established by international treaties. Reportedly, treatment can include daily 6-hour questioning sessions, no access to lawyers, no access to exercise, confinement in small cells packed beyond capacity, and lights that stay on 24 hours a day.

Together, these secretive characteristics paint a hazy picture of the agency's operations and activities. From the information that is known, one thing is clear: China's spying operates very differently than that of Western countries and very differently than what appears on the big screen.

China's system of government is an authoritarian one, which means it requires strict obedience from its citizens. China focuses greatly on keeping complete control over its political power within its borders. Sometimes this means trying to control what people think and how they act to protect the government from internal revolutions and uprisings.

Tiananmen Square in Beijing has deep cultural, historical, and political importance for China. In the spring of 1989, thousands of people gathered there to demand political reform, greater freedom of speech, and an end to government corruption. Eventually, millions of people joined the protests. This posed an immediate and serious threat to the CCP, which responded by sending ground troops and military tanks in to stop the uprising. Deadly clashes occurred between soldiers and protesters. The exact number of casualties remains unclear, but estimates range from hundreds to several thousand.

Uprisings such as the Tiananmen Square protests presented a new kind of threat to the Chinese government—one of ideas and cultural movements that stood in the way of the CCP's goals. Instead of worrying about military attacks from other countries , the CCP became increasingly concerned about foreigners teaming up with people inside the country to try to undermine the government. Largely in response to the events of 1989,

China updated its constitution in 1993 to include the State Security Law. The law was designed to increase state control and prevent future uprisings. It was also intended to combat threats originating from outside China.

The State Security Law gives the Chinese government great power to crack down on dissent and tighten

Protest in Tiananmen Square

its grip on society in general. Furthermore, Article 16 requires all citizens and organizations to assist in state security work. This means that every Chinese citizen and every Chinese company is obligated to help the government meet its state security goals, whatever those goals may be. The MSS is the agency in charge of enforcing these laws.

The view most Chinese citizens have of their government differs from the view most citizens of Western countries have of theirs. This is in large part due to the Chinese social credit system. This system keeps track of what people do, and it gives them a score. People are scored on things such as online behavior, financial activities, employment status, personal characteristics, and education. If someone has a high score, they get more benefits. They may get easier access to loans or travel permits. But if their score is low, they could face penalties or restrictions. This system makes people want to behave in ways the government approves of. It also helps the government keep control over what people do and think, including whether they might be willing to spy.

Scholars outside China agree that the PRC defines intelligence practices quite differently than most Western countries. Anyone who is considered a dissident can be locked up without trial and without access to a lawyer. This practice is intended to keep people from speaking out against the Chinese government. Knowing the potential consequences of their words, scholars inside China face serious limitations on what they can publish about Chinese intelligence, leaving very little exposed from within the country.

投票箱

Mao Zedong [*left*] was a persuasive leader who easily convinced Chinese citizens to spy on each other.

China is the first modern power to use its entire society as a means for gathering intelligence. As a result, Chinese tactics are often unrecognizable compared to other countries. Some of the common tradecraft, such as encrypted messages and **dead drops**, are practically non-existent in modern Chinese spying. Instead, the Chinese rely on an abundance of espionage operations that are conducted by regular citizens and spies alike. They also seem to have very different priorities compared to the Western powers. The Chinese rely heavily on stealing information on things such as new technologies and weapons systems. This includes stealing intellectual property on everything from 5G networks and jet engines to explosives and cell phone technology. This practice is called intellectual espionage, also known as economic espionage or industrial espionage.

Intellectual espionage involves secretly obtaining valuable information or ideas, typically for economic or strategic advantage. China, like many other nations, operates a significant espionage network. This includes the use of its citizens traveling abroad to gather intelligence for the government or for Chinese companies. This might entail methods such as **cyberattacks** or hiring insiders to disclose non-public information. This can enhance China's competitiveness on the global stage. However, intellectual espionage is illegal and can strain international relations between China and its allies and enemies alike. Senior U.S. law enforcement officials have publicly identified China as "the most active foreign power engaged in illegal acquisition of American technology."

The Chinese government uses many methods to secretly get its citizens to help gather information and support its goals. One way is by pressuring people into spying, sometimes by threatening them or their families if they don't cooperate. Also, they use a lot of surveillance, such as cameras and Internet monitoring, to keep an eye on what people are doing online and in public places. Much of this surveillance can have a direct effect on an individual's social credit rating.

Additionally, the government uses businesses and organizations it owns to gather ever more information on its own citizens. Employees might be asked to report on their coworkers or customers without them realizing it. There are also entire networks of people who report on others, watching for anything the government considers risky, dangerous, or potentially threatening to the CCP's power structure.

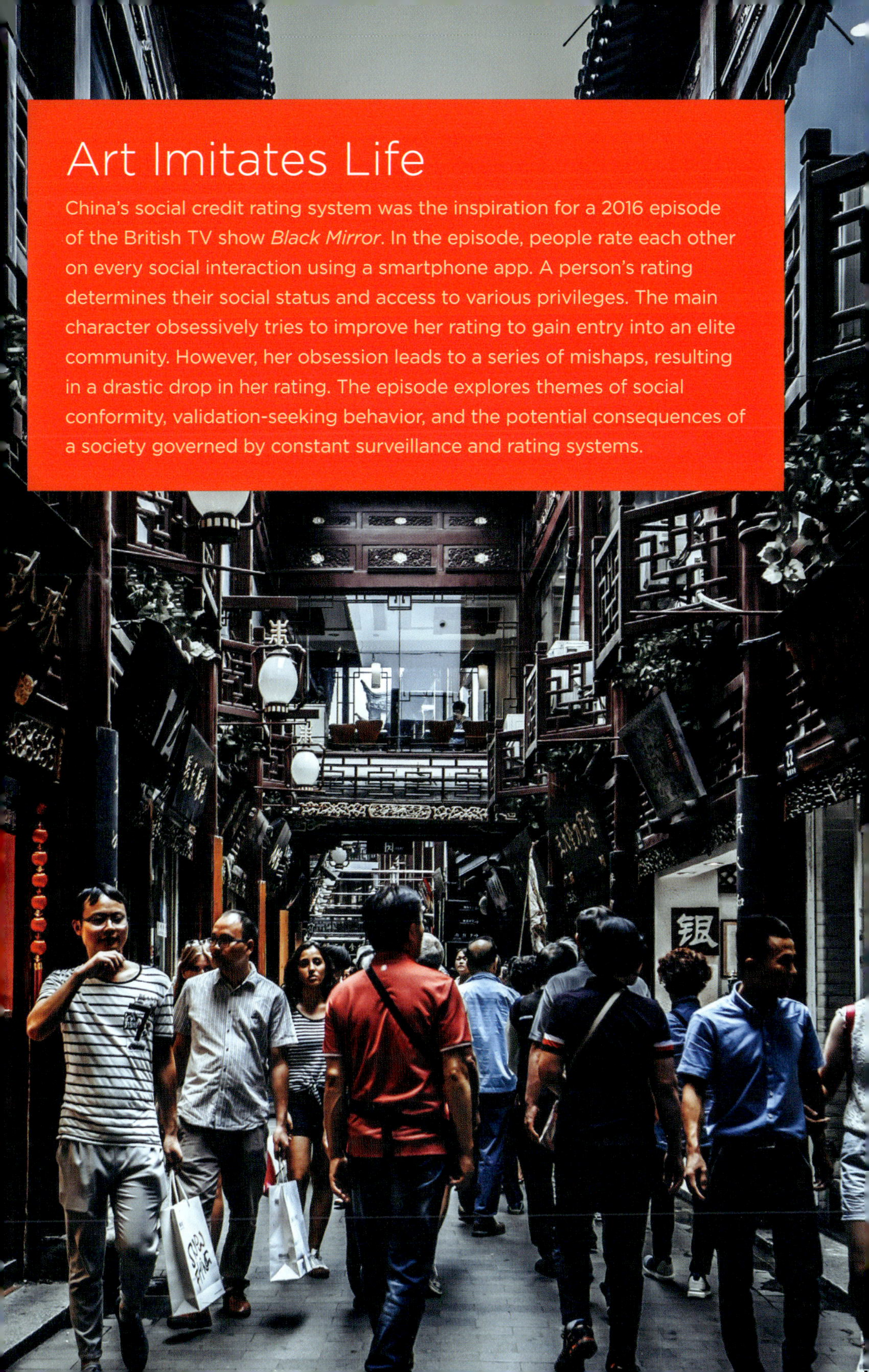

Art Imitates Life

China's social credit rating system was the inspiration for a 2016 episode of the British TV show *Black Mirror*. In the episode, people rate each other on every social interaction using a smartphone app. A person's rating determines their social status and access to various privileges. The main character obsessively tries to improve her rating to gain entry into an elite community. However, her obsession leads to a series of mishaps, resulting in a drastic drop in her rating. The episode explores themes of social conformity, validation-seeking behavior, and the potential consequences of a society governed by constant surveillance and rating systems.

In schools and universities, students and teachers are often pressured to report on each other if they see or hear something that goes against what the government wants. The government also tries to get information from Chinese people living in other countries, using their connections and relationships to learn about what's happening abroad.

Overall, the MSS's activities on the global stage reflect China's growing assertiveness and ambitions as a major world power. Its operations have raised concerns among foreign governments and international organizations about espionage, computer-related threats, and the broader implications for global security and stability. As China continues to expand its influence and capabilities, the role of the MSS in shaping global affairs is likely to remain a subject of scrutiny and debate.

Tools of the Trade(craft)

Ancient China and much of Asia saw widespread use of spies and espionage during its turbulent history. These **operatives** mastered the art of tradecraft. They wore disguises and took on various roles such as merchants or scholars to seamlessly blend into their surroundings.

Ties on Spies

Sometimes the tools of the trade of spycraft are simple, everyday objects. In a famous case from the 1970s, the object was a necktie. When a supposed trade delegation from China visited France and was shown secret chemicals used in developing photographs, French authorities witnessed some odd behavior. Members of the delegation were seen dipping the tips of their ties into trays containing the chemicals. It was suspected that they were trying to collect samples of the chemicals to transport back to China for analysis.

Spies communicated through secret codes and messages. To do this, they used a network of informants strategically positioned in key locations. Great skill was required to avoid detection and deceive enemies. Secrecy was always a top priority.

Communication was crucial for coordinating movements and sharing important information. Chinese spies used many ancient signaling methods to communicate, including beacon fires, smoke signals, drumbeats, signal flags, and semaphore. Spies also used homing pigeons to carry messages. They set up signal stations, watchtowers, and relay stations along strategic routes and borders to quickly send messages over long distances. To make sure these messages were understood correctly, they used standardized codes, signals, and procedures. This helped prevent mistakes and keep communication efficient.

Skills even extended to stealthy movement and lock-picking, allowing spies to move discreetly and access secured areas unnoticed. When the situation called for it, they would damage or destroy their enemies' critical infrastructure such as bridges and factories. These historical espionage techniques highlight the creativity and resourcefulness of Chinese spies in their quest for information and advantage. However, many of these practices fell out of use as espionage moved into the modern era.

Part of a spy's job is to transfer information as quietly and elusively as possible.

Since its beginning in 1949, the PRC has been engaged in espionage. However, little is known about its modern spying methods, tools, personnel, or its basic organization. The MSS has had fewer **defectors** compared to most other intelligence services around the world. That means there have not been many individuals to share the agency's secrets.

Russia's KGB, in operation from 1954 to 1991, frequently worked with desperate sources who needed money. The idea was that they were easier to control since they were vulnerable. However, China prefers to make spies out of trusted, upstanding members of society. That keeps them from appearing suspicious when traveling, working, and living abroad. The MSS also does not always pay large sums of money for even the most sensitive materials. In one example, a man's reward for more than 20 years' worth of espionage in the United States was simply a guarantee that his sick mother-in-law would receive proper medical attention.

The MSS trains its operatives over long periods of time—sometimes many years. And it trains so many people, sends so many spies out into the world, that even if just a few of them are eventually able to provide valuable information, the CCP will see it as a win. The Chinese government does not favor a short-term approach. It prefers to take the long approach and is very patient to let the information it desires come to light naturally. There is one account of a Chinese secret agent who waited in Canada for 24 years before ever being given a mission. This is not surprising for a civilization that built more than 10,000 miles (16,093 kilometers) of the Great Wall of China more than 2,000 years ago and that had whole libraries of printed books decades before the invention of the printing press in Europe.

Furthermore, China likes to employ people who truly are who they say they are. They don't pretend to be someone else. A spy who says she is a journalist or a scientist really is a journalist or scientist. Chinese spies blend in easily because they're not lying. This makes it very hard for security services in other countries to catch them. That said, there are exceptions to this rule. In one case, Chinese intelligence officers spent years training a man how to be a Roman Catholic priest. They made

sure that he had a perfect cover so that he could blend in and avoid detection. His job was to act as a contact and courier for Larry Wu-tai Chin, an infamous Chinese spy.

By comparison, Western and Russian intelligence agents often use fake identities. They try to quickly get

OPPOSITE The Internet is fertile ground for countless Chinese spies.

their hands on the sensitive materials or documents they are after. They then meet up at a safe house or have a dead drop in a certain location. Sometimes they will use secret communication networks to make transfers to their handlers. Then it's time for "extracting" the agent, which means getting them safely out of harm's way.

Western intelligence officers would view using students as spies as far too risky. However, Chinese officers are thought to use students frequently in intelligence gathering. It is estimated that as many as 300,000 Chinese undergraduate students are studying in the United States. It is further estimated that 10 percent of them, or 30,000, will visit sensitive sites with their schools in various class groups and on tours. If even just a few of them can learn any secrets and bring them back home to China, the CCP will view it as a victory.

Sometimes it is not an individual who is asked to spy by the CCP. It can be an entire business organization. Much like the Chinese spies who really are who they say they are, a Chinese business operating overseas blends in and avoids detection because it truly is a successfully operating business.

The life of a spy in most TV shows and Hollywood movies is action-packed and filled with high-stakes drama. Spies such as Jason Bourne and James Bond arm themselves with fancy gadgets, jet-powered cars, and futuristic technology. Tom Cruise's Ethan Hunt character in the *Mission: Impossible* movies leaps from an airplane, scales skyscrapers and sheer canyon walls, and drives a motorcycle off a cliff. Although today's MSS agents are shrouded in secrecy, their lives certainly have very little in common with these fictional spies.

Keeping It Real

Traditional spy films often emphasize high-tech gadgets, disguises, and glamorous settings. In contrast, the 2020 action movie *Mulan* presents a more realistic take on espionage, especially within the context of Chinese history and culture. In the movie, Mulan disguises herself as a man to take her father's place in the army. Throughout the story, she must use her intelligence and skills to protect China from invading forces, effectively acting as a spy within the enemy ranks. The film highlights tactics such as deception, observation, and strategic thinking. These are indeed more closely aligned with historical practices of espionage and intelligence gathering.

Unveiling MSS Missions

The MSS is an extremely powerful organization with vague limitations on its power. It has far fewer budgetary concerns than Western intelligence agencies. Its tactics are persistent and ever-changing, and there is a deep loyalty woven throughout the agency. However, the MSS does not exist in a vacuum. There are instances where the true identities of those acting as agents for the MSS have been discovered. One such case is that of Larry Wu-tai Chin.

OPPOSITE: After receiving a life sentence for spying, Larry Wu-tai Chin said, "It was worth it. I have nothing to regret."

Larry Wu-tai Chin was employed by the CIA as a translator during the 1940s. Chin was **recruited** in 1948 to spy for China. During the course of 30 years, he covertly sent sensitive information to Chinese handlers while advancing his career within the CIA. He eventually became a CIA intelligence analyst with top-secret clearance. He made regular trips to international locations such as Toronto, Hong Kong, and London. There, he would meet with contacts to exchange classified documents and information. This included details about U.S. activities in Asia, especially during the Korean War (1950–53) and the Vietnam War (1955–75), helping China understand U.S. foreign policy and military capabilities. Chin remained undetected until his 1985 arrest by the U.S. Federal Bureau of Investigation (FBI). His case made U.S. intelligence agencies rethink how to keep the country safe. As time went on, the type of information gathered by the MSS changed. It shifted away from sweeping, large-scale war-time political and military intentions. The information being collected became less general and more specific.

Yu Enguang, an MSS operative, initially served as a reporter for Xinhua (the New China News Agency) in London during the 1970s. He later moved to Washington, D.C., where he covered the Carter and Reagan presidential administrations. When he returned to Beijing in 1988, Yu assumed a new role at the China International Culture Exchange Center. This organization, suspected to be backed by the MSS, provided him with opportunities for more espionage activities.

While publicly living one life, Yu was secretly spying for the MSS. His work involved **infiltrating**

OPPOSITE Li Fengzhi is a former MSS spy who became disillusioned with his work and sought refuge in the United States.

foreign businesses and organizations to gather classified information about various aspects of national security. When a large leak of financial documents happened in 2017, Yu was named as the director of a company operating in Bermuda. Intelligence analysts eventually grew suspicious that the individual named "Yu" in the leaked financial documents and the "Yu" known to work for the MSS were, in fact, the same person. This was later proven with photographic evidence.

Sometimes the MSS is involved in seemingly minor cultural events. At other times, things are much more complex, as in the case of Bin Wu. His story is an elaborate tale of espionage and betrayal. Wu was a double agent operating within both the FBI and the MSS. He was initially hired by the FBI to provide information on Chinese espionage activities. However, in 1992, his double-agent status was uncovered when it was revealed that he was secretly sending high-tech components, such as tubes used in night vision scopes, back to the MSS. This act compromised U.S. national security and led to his arrest and conviction. However, there's more to the story.

Wu claimed he was forced into his role as a spy for China. He said that happened when the Chinese government learned he was a pro-democracy activist. This raised questions about his true motivations and loyalties. It also meant that U.S. authorities had to figure out if he was a double agent or a triple agent, meaning that he was actually working for the MSS the whole time and was just pretending to work for the FBI. Either way, Wu faced the threat of deportation back to China, where he feared that he would be tortured and executed. In an effort to avoid that fate, he sought political **asylum** in the United States. "They will kill one to warn a hundred," Wu said.

Ironically, Wu sought asylum through the very agency he was accused of betraying, the FBI. But not all who seek asylum do so after being caught. In the late 2000s, an MSS officer named Li Fengzhi defected to the United States. He revealed that China's spy service spends much time stealing secrets abroad and suppressing dissent at home. He also said that the most important mission of the MSS is to maintain Communist Party control; that the MSS is deeply involved in repressing certain religious groups and dissenters within China; that the MSS censors the Internet in China to control the flow of information; and that the MSS targets non-state-sanctioned religious groups and pro-democracy activists.

Defections from the MSS are rare. Li defected due to his dissatisfaction with the Communist Party's actions against its own people. He hoped his defection would lead to large-scale political and social change within China. Li emphasized that a government that mistreats its people cannot stay stable. He urged the West not to seek economic and political gains from doing business with China while simultaneously ignoring human rights abuses.

It is not always Chinese nationals who end up spying for the MSS. Kevin Mallory, a U.S. citizen and former CIA officer, was convicted in 2018 of spying for the PRC. His involvement with Chinese intelligence began in 2017. He was recruited by Chinese agents during a trip to Shanghai. Over the following months, he sent classified documents and information to his handlers, believing he was acting in China's interests. Mallory's actions mirrored those of earlier spies such as Larry Wu-tai Chin, highlighting the persistence and ongoing adaptability of foreign intelligence efforts. U.S. authorities eventually uncovered Mallory's

Andrew Ridgeley [*left*] and George Michael, the pop duo Wham!

Setting the Stage

During the late 1980s, China was undergoing Deng Xiaoping's reform and "opening-up policy." The MSS played a role in enabling Julio Iglesias to make history as the first Western entertainer to perform live on Chinese television. Another notable instance involved a photograph capturing George Michael, of the music group Wham!, alongside Wang Shuren, a prominent Chinese intelligence officer, at a banquet hosted for Wham! in China. This suggests the agency's involvement in diplomatic and cultural events to further their objectives. It also hints at an effort by the CCP to present China as a modern superpower that embraces Western culture.

activities, leading to his arrest and conviction. Despite his background in intelligence and knowledge of the risks, Mallory fell victim to the allure of financial gain.

Money is not always a reason people give for spying. Sometimes they do it just because it is good for the country. Such was the case for Edward Peng, a Chinese intelligence officer with the MSS. In October 2018, he was arrested and sent from Belgium to the United States to face trial. He was accused of attempting to commit economic espionage. Specifically, he wanted to steal technology secrets from multiple U.S. aviation and aerospace companies to give China military advantages and economic gain. Peng's task was to recruit employees of U.S. companies to gather sensitive information for the MSS. He got the information in several ways, including bribery, threats, and hacking. Peng also tried to get employees from these companies to travel to China. He wanted them to go under the false pretense of delivering presentations at universities. In November 2022, Peng was proven guilty and sentenced to 20 years in prison.

Alexander Yuk Ching Ma, a former CIA officer, was arrested in August 2020 for espionage. He was accused of working with one of his relatives to pass secret information to the MSS. Ma worked for the CIA for several years before settling in Hawaii, where he later joined the FBI as a language expert. He allegedly leaked information for more than 10 years, starting with meetings in Hong Kong in 2001. Ma faced charges of plotting to communicate U.S. national defense secrets to aid a foreign government. In 2021, he was sentenced to 20 years in prison for his actions.

11:31
TikTok

Ancient Secrets, Modern Methods

The MSS has one clear mission: safeguarding the CCP's political security. Initially, its focus was on traditional intelligence gathering, counterespionage, and maintaining internal security. Since then, technological advancements, including the dawn of the Internet, have given way to an age dominated by information.

OPPOSITE: The popular app TikTok has been suspected as an intelligence-gathering device, due to its Chinese ties.

The expansion of the Internet throughout the 1990s and early 2000s marked the beginning of the modern digital age. The Internet transformed society, communication, commerce, and countless other aspects of modern life. This has led to a shift in priorities for the types of intelligence the MSS gathers. This is evidenced by the massive number of Chinese espionage cases that have come to light since the start of the 21st century.

Since 2012, when Xi Jinping became the president of China, espionage priorities seem to have shifted again. When Xi assumed office, he updated China's intelligence collection priorities to better serve long-term goals. In 2017, President Xi said he wanted a fully modernized military by 2035 and a world-class military by the middle of the 21st century. To achieve these goals, Xi put an end to data collection that was for personal gain—meaning, intelligence gathered for the sole purpose of making money. The MSS started focusing more on large goals related to national security and global politics and increased its cyberespionage (computer-related spying) efforts.

One example of alleged cyberespionage occurred between 2010 and 2015. Ten MSS intelligence officers and computer hackers were accused of stealing airline engine technology from companies working together in France and the United States. The aim of the espionage was to obtain intellectual property and confidential information related to jet engine technology. China's defense industry is now reportedly developing a similar engine.

In another example, Chinese hackers infiltrated a U.S. contractor working with the Navy. Before the theft was detected, 614 gigabytes of information were stolen. Included were materials related to a supersonic anti-ship missile intended for use on U.S. submarines. Also stolen were submarine radio room specifications related to coding systems and the Navy Submarine Development Unit's electronic warfare library.

On January 28, 2023, the United States detected a balloon carrying a large payload of cargo flying through its airspace. The balloon traveled over Alaska, through Canada, and across the middle of the continental United States. In February 2023, it was shot down by a U.S. fighter jet off the coast of Myrtle Beach, South Carolina. Initially, U.S. officials said the balloon was Chinese in origin and designed as a tool for espionage. They said it had sent data to Beijing but that its purpose was unclear. Chinese officials, meanwhile, stated that the balloon's journey into U.S. airspace was an accident and that the balloon was, in fact, a tool for measuring weather conditions.

The 2023 Chinese balloon, as seen from a U.S. military plane

Chinese president Xi Jinping

The balloon incident triggered a significant dispute between the United States and China. It led to the cancellation of a planned trip to China by the U.S. Secretary of State, Anthony Blinken. It also caused a notable increase in tensions between the two superpowers. The wreckage of the balloon was retrieved from the bottom of the Atlantic Ocean by the U.S. Navy. General Mark Milley of the U.S. Army clarified months later that the balloon wasn't involved in spying or gathering intelligence. Instead, it likely drifted off course due to strong winds at the high altitudes where the balloon flew. Even though the wreckage of the balloon revealed that its sensors were indeed inactive while over the United States, suspicions about potential espionage activities lingered.

President Joe Biden acknowledged the incident and highlighted its negative impact on relations between the United States and China. The event served as a reminder of the delicate nature of international relations and the potential consequences that even seemingly minor incidents can have.

In addition to the MSS, enterprises owned or partially owned by the Chinese government are also engaged in intelligence gathering. In 2018, President Xi directed all state-owned enterprises, such as certains banks, construction companies, and insurance agencies, to change their rules. The change directed them to officially emphasize serving the CCP and protecting the country's security over making money. These enterprises frequently engage in cyberespionage, often targeting key industries such as defense, aerospace, pharmaceuticals, and technology research. Nearly half of China's espionage activities target U.S. military and space technologies, while about 25 percent focus on commercial interests. Despite international scrutiny and arrests, China shows no signs of slowing down its espionage efforts.

Another top priority of the MSS is to maintain the CCP's control of Chinese citizens living in China. One new way in which they exercise this control is through the "Counterespionage Law of the People's Republic of China," which was enacted in 2023. The law emphasizes the need for both specialized agencies and the collective effort of the public to fight espionage. It states that all parts of society must participate in preventing espionage and protecting national interests. This includes training and raising public awareness through education. The law also bans the transfer of any information related to national security. The definition of "espionage" now includes the phrase "documents, data, materials or items related to national security and interests," without specifying how those terms are defined.

Additionally, the 2023 law introduces a system of rewards and protections for individuals and organizations who help the counterespionage efforts. The timing of this law lined up with the MSS creating an account on the Chinese social media platform WeChat. The agency has used the WeChat account to launch manga-style comics and videos to address national security and espionage threats. These comics depict real counterespionage cases, aiming to raise awareness about national security. They encourage alerting authorities to suspicious behavior and list phone numbers and websites where people can report their suspicions.

Beijing has been using cartoons for decades to get its message across. The 1980s cartoon *Black Cat Detective* has had a remake for the digital age. Now *Black Cat Detective* tackles cybersecurity and hackers. Through extensive media attention and engagement on platforms such as WeChat, the MSS is creatively involving citizens in anti-spying operations.

The MSS has evolved significantly since its founding in 1983. Its activities now encompass a wide range of strategic objectives, including both traditional intelligence gathering and cyberoperations. The impact of Chinese espionage remains significant, affecting not only the global economy but also global security and global stability.

Cyberattack

Operation Aurora is a notable cyberattack that happened in 2010 and was traced back to China. The cyberattacks targeted corporate networks of giant firms such as Google, Adobe, and Yahoo to get valuable intellectual property and gather intelligence. The action had the potential to undermine the competitiveness and security of the affected organizations and give an advantage to Chinese corporations and the CCP. Google's willingness to talk about the attack raised awareness of cybersecurity threats. It also prompted widespread improvements to security measures. In response, Google began emphasizing strict access control and user verification.

Selected Bibliography

Eftimiades, Nicholas. *Chinese Intelligence Operations.* Arlington, Va.: Newcomb Publishers, 1998.

---. "Uncovering Chinese Espionage in the U.S." *The Diplomat.* November 28, 2018. https://thediplomat.com/2018/11/uncovering-chinese-espionage-in-the-us.

Joske, Alex. *Spies and Lies: How China's Greatest Covert Operations Fooled the World.* Richmond, Victoria: Hardie Grant Books, 2022.

Leahy, Joe. "China's Feared Spy Agency Steps Out of the Shadows." *Financial Times.* January 22, 2024. https://www.ft.com/content/f78c7243-2ff5-4f77-93d0-91c20f6b5548.

Mattis, Peter L., and Matthew J. Brazil. *Chinese Communist Espionage: An Intelligence Primer.* Annapolis, Md.: Naval Institute Press, 2019.

Smith, I. C., and Nigel West. *Historical Dictionary of Chinese Intelligence.* Lanham, Md.: Rowman & Littlefield, 2021.

Zhang, Laney. "China: Counteresionage Law Revised." Library of Congress. September 22, 2023. https://www.loc.gov/item/global-legal-monitor/2023-09-21/china-counterespionage-law-revised.

Glossary

agent a person who works for, but is not necessarily officially employed by, an intelligence service

asylum protection and safety given by one country to someone fleeing danger in another country

communist related to a political and economic system in which all goods and property are owned by the state and shared by all members of the public

counterespionage efforts made by a nation's intelligence agency to catch and eliminate spies working against the country and protect the country against sabotage or terrorism; also called counterintelligence

covert undercover or hidden

cyberattack an attempt to gain illegal access to a computer or computer network for the purpose of causing damage or harm

dead drop a prearranged spot for dropping off and picking up information gathered through spying

defector someone who leaves a country forever in favor of another

dissent	to disagree to the level of rebellion, usually against a government
double agent	a spy for one country who doubles as a spy for a second country and often provides false information to the first country
encryption	the process of turning something into a code
espionage	the act of spying
imperial dynasty	a type of government used by an empire in which leadership succession is based on heredity
infiltrate	to secretly enter in a gradual way, usually for the purpose of spying
intelligence	information uncovered and transmitted by a spy
monarchy	a form of government in which one person, usually a king or queen, rules, having achieved the title through heredity
operative	an undercover agent working for an intelligence agency
recruit	to hire or enlist
surveillance	the act of keeping close watch on something or someone
tradecraft	the procedures, techniques, and devices used by spies to carry out their activities

Websites

China

https://www.cia.gov/the-world-factbook/countries/china
Learn facts about China's geography, people, economy, and more.

The International Spy Museum

https://www.spymuseum.org
Explore frequently asked questions about spying and bios of real-life agents.

Sun Tzu on the Art of War

https://sites.ualberta.ca/~enoch/Readings/The_Art_Of_War.pdf
Read a translation of Sun Tzu's classic written work about military strategy.

Index